POWER THROUGH

POWER THROUGH

Poems For Manly Men
By a Manly Man

Zanzibar "Buck Buck" McFate

NMPAA Approved*

*The National Men's Poetry Association of America

iUniverse, Inc.
New York Lincoln Shanghai

Power Through
Poems For Manly Men By a Manly Man

iUniverse books may be ordered through booksellers or by contacting:

iUniverse
2021 Pine Lake Road, Suite 100
Lincoln, NE 68512
www.iuniverse.com
1-800-Authors (1-800-288-4677)

ISBN: 978-0-595-43911-9 (pbk)

ISBN: 978-0-595-88233-5 (ebk)

Printed in the United States of America

Virtus Semper Viridis

Goodness will find the little boy.
It always has. It always will.

—Cormac McCarthy
The Road

Contents

-er 1

CATACOMBS 2

POSEURS 6

BODIE-BO-DO-HODIE-HEY! 10

EXECUTIONS 12

CLYDE 'N' PLOOT 14

THEN I DO! 15

I GOT HEART PAIN 17

HAVING FAILED 19

ENVY 20

CONCEIT 21

I HAVE A BIBLE 22

SPREAD THE GOSPEL 24

PROSTATE EXAM 26

"HOW PAINTBRUSHES ARE LIKE PANTIES" 27

SWIMMER 35

SOMETIMES I TRY 37

CHOCOLATE BOX 39

SCROTUNDRUM 41

BOXING 42

HANDLER 43

RHYMER 44

VANITY PLATE 47

THREE LIMERICKS 49

THE CHALLENGE 50

THE SERMON 51

REPRIEVE 53

THE SWEET (STING OF) LIFE 54

EIGHT TABLESPOONS 56

A PROMINENT DAIRY AIR 58

IT'S HARD TO SAY 60

VIRGINIA HAM 61

CORRECTING ELAINE 63

REMINDER 64

THE VERY THOUGHT OF LOSING IS HATEFUL 65

LIKE TIGERS AFTER PANCAKES 68

I AM ON MARS 70

-er

-er Propell I into sauntered a
Sliced all me way to the Parsnippany
(fay, Pravor me a bit and so say it it with rhymes "a.")
Ten thoured hunsand thru-see azzip cakepan me's
And to the Parrens Bine of Nouth sJ
Pist Pascataway, nwod to obileM Bay
To south San east Jose of Alabam
a! Lord, was I cut panstrarent thin
loating drifty F pon ze hyr air's 's fairju
Scant as a y French jellyooh—fish's under la theres
put back to be again together Never
Win some of me slipped through a dow
in a pan landed and was countryfied
r One taste me and you'd like to of a died
More of me, indingclu a liver of sliver and a piece of knee
Drifted sound cartilage less less ly ly to the Cabirbean Sea
Whereapairl of obsters named M M oe and arie ate me dainty
With fisdigured wripshecked orphan out-your-eyes-cry her balmintsea grasstea.
The rest, I guess, spun counterantigraviclockesiw
And öh wirled flyign saucre styel throuhg the No sphere
Past ars, the Masteroid bel t,and frozeon peNtune's ethanem sniat nuom
It's a a shme that I'm s p r e a d t h i n
But tha t's the kind of shapes I'm in—
dewercS.

CATACOMBS

Tentacles, tin men, and lasses in tight T's—
All these and more by tempting tease:

> I walk in vast candlelit corridors of the past
> —Walls sweat memories interred—
> Preposterous catacomb concatenations
> Bones, selves on shelves unglued.

This is where Nazis rocked.
Listen to cavern echoes of Nazi rock.
Ya! Boots-a-go-go!
God has lost! Los! Los! Los!
Gottlos! Gottlos! Gottlos! Go!

Doris Day licks the shine off der Führer's buttery tapping toes.
Dinah Shore pogos. Pat Boone's a'mosh.
The Babe's goosestepping 'round third,
And me? I'm eating Cassius Clay's whole smokin' tongue
On a cold slab of chewy Jewy rye.
Wasted, I use the toilet backwards.

I am feeling an overwhelming lassitude.
(Maybe it's 'cuz the lass got nude.)
Cannibalism? It's in. It's here to stay.
I'm telling you, my friend, it's the way I play.

> What can you prove with your point?
> What do you gain by sticking it
> In, in, in, and in again?

Do you believe or were you aware
That giving advice can be inappropriate
And not even nice?

Marion Crane's jitterbugging with Wo Fat.
Sugar, push! Cherry, drop! Frankie, snatch! Trip out, Jack!
Hobo chairman's cracking a sausage whip,
Flickin' off that ashen maid's white satin slip.

    I feel an affinity for the mad.
    I, too, sometime would like to defused be,
    Sprayed—squeeze, bang—out
    The end of a poor rich lady's artillery tube.

    'tis peace:
    The rock suspended in air.

And fall down Jill? I found the pebble in her quarry.
She wanted a new inning,
For me to crack her up.
I gave it to her—boom boom boom—
I had her graveling everywhere.
With cream, it's serene.

Boom! Bang!
Let's Nazi! Nazi Rock! Ya! Yeah!
Hoppe! Hoppe! Spring!

    A pink moment
    On a wild clear afternoon—
    The smell of Lincoln Logs,

Yet Whistler's Mother's macabre
Crosslegged clutching a crozier
In her Adirondack chair,
The mill house crook between her legs.
And it's a bumpy black buggy ride
With an iron kettle of black human dye.
Once I kick down the red door,
She and I shall paint the sky.

Nazi! Nazi! Rock! Rock! Rock!
Raus! Rein! Go! Go! Go!

Chunks of debris fall rudely from the chapel wall.
The statues of saints all run and hide.
Little Bo Peep's hearing chin music.
Quakin' Abe rubs his Brillo pad between her feet.
Lick a chicky-chick's drumstick!
Do the Nazi! Nazi Rock! Yeah!

> What is the weight of blood?
> Exactly what is the specific gravity of the contents of your head?

> Every window in my house is broken.
> Men hammer nails into eggs into the street,
> Thus are swans punished for being indiscreet.
> Shoats and sows splay on the curb, masturbating.
> Moses sleeps underneath his yeasty canoe.

What a big, horny carny bore he is!

> All I see is dust ahead, dragster fire to my rear.
> I don't know what to do.

Do the Nazi! Nazi! Yeah! Yeah! Yeah!

I love the pepper smell of dirt.
I rub a mango in my armpit.
I like it because it fits.

Tied up, in the bondage of your hair,
I lost the joint of my middle finger.
It was boudoir gunplay antics.
I was flippin' you the bird, Goldilocks, and away my trigger flew.
Ask me if I care.

> Without fruit, without sin:
> Lady Vampire, say, "Amen."

In a warren of thorns
My eyes fell in firepit ashes.
On my knees I seek them again
Gripped in mitt of Michigan.
Through synthesis I achieve
A picture with a pen.

I bowl with my poet friends on a long hollow open road.
Waves snap trees. Colors scream.
Listen within yourself, my fair lady, and what do you see?
An open frame? A mouth that moans?
Is that you, Madonna, in the gutter balling?
I see the scarlet halo scarf with which you so silkily sin;
Trees blob, and red vines take Audrey Hepburn
As she runs red unbuttoned down the stairs,
A hairy hound of Budapest never leaving her alone.

O, great all-pervasive pestilential moon,
Reach your tentacle rays!
Encoil and ravish me do,
Like in a dream of the fisherman's wife.
Eerie shadows drenched in moonlight.
Are they two, three, ten men?
[… Made to commit acts too unspeakable to be stated here …]
Red queen teases in a black leotard
A carp to entangle in her fishnets.

I don't want your pity.

I don't want your lamb.
I sure as Sam don't want your Korean Ho Jon sucking Spam.

I fear.
In pure radiant light beams
The rock is suspended.

Alles is gut. Alles schläft.

POSEURS

a)

I want to center you
Here
In your dressing room
With my camera.

Pose
Or not.
Just be
Natural. Real.

I want you
Doing your hair.
Do your maquillage.
Mah key—ahs.

Love your fuzzy …
So déshabillé
Or as you say in English—
Dish-able. A peach pie.

Flower: garden: woman.
Like photo. One. Same.
All require close cropping.
I am so weeding you.

I embarrass you.
Has anyone ever told you
You have the most
Beautiful breasts?

Your mother!
Someone loves you.
They are festive.
A virgin's.

That is the dress.
Pretty pleats,
Folds and gathers.
Very you.

I have a sculptor friend,
A real Michaelangelo.
He could be your lover.
I could let you have him.

Be complicit now.
Think about who you are doing.
You are mad. Mad!
Mad with a graceful mien.

Dark. Drowsy. Detached.
Apprehensive. Shattered.
You are between customers
In a Brazilian brothel.

You are Christ-like.
Show me your stigmata.
O, agony.
Pierced by a spear.

We are in la boucherie.
Three lambs' heads—
Tongues like this …
They want to hang with you.

Nice shoes.

b)

I want to center you
Here
In your dressing room
With my camera.

Pose
Or not.
Just be
Natural. Real.

I want you
Doing your hair.
Do your maquillage.
Mah key—ahs.

Love your fuzzy …
So déshabillé
Or as you say in English—
Dish-able. A peach pie.

Flower: garden: woman.
Like photo. One. Same.
All require close cropping.
I am so weeding you.

I embarrass you.
Has anyone ever told you
You have the most
Beautiful breasts?

Your mother!
Someone loves you.
They are festive.
A virgin's.

That is the dress.
Pretty pleats,
Folds and gathers.
Very you.

I have a sculptor friend,
A real Michaelangelo.
He could be your lover.
I could let you have him.

Be complicit now.
Think about who you are doing.
You are mad. Mad!
Mad with a graceful mien.

Dark. Drowsy. Detached.
Apprehensive. Shattered.
You are between customers
In a Brazilian brothel.

You are Christ-like.
Show me your stigmata.
O, agony.
Pierced by a spear.

We are in la boucherie.
Three lambs' heads—
Tongues like this ...
They want to hang with you.

Nice shoes.

Yes, I put the kids to bed.

BODIE-BO-DO-HODIE-HEY!

God's got a hundred-thousand-million road-map weary eyes,
He rides the streets of Laredo, a cowboy go-to-meeting disguised.
He wears white linen Levis with silver buckle shoes.
He wields a cast-iron smitin' fish, He oldtestamentally knows how to use.
He's got a dazzling earring. The Old Boy's mostly bald.
He stands a full ten-feet 'n' six in rattler heels 'n' all.
He's got a gold tooth incisor that glows sunfire awe-full fine,
And a tattoo of the universe down where the sun does never shine.
God drives a pick-up, and He don't pesterate the stick.
It's a modern-day shepherd's rod, and He shifts her smooth and quick.
He don't sport no brand new pink trim fin showroom Cadillac,
But, brother, I tell you what—There ain't nothing the Lord don't lack.
Right about now, He's percolatin' to the all-nite neon Mojo Mart,
Looking for a paperback treatise by a Frenchie named Descartes.
His one-eyed hound, Billie Jo, is snoring curled in back.
One eye shut, one open—that's a Natural Law Biblicious fact.
Locked in His steely glove box, God's got a rolled-up scroll
For when His Final Thunder Boom 'n' Doom Hour tolls
Recite shall He His set-in-stone Santa-type eternal judgment list.
O, brother, some will seethe in pain, but some will rise like mist.
I tell you what—God's smokin' Luckies, no cancer risk for He.
Listen, Sinners—My Fiery Tribulation! L.S.M.F.T!
God enjoys a taste of fiery spirits now and sometimes again.
If He rampages, as in Noah's time, best notify your next of kin.
On the rack behind and, of course, above him rest
Instruments of obedience whose deliverance is blest:
A faithful, well-oiled Remington 30 zero six
For to keep puppet-mouth demons from playing sinning tricks;
There also hangs a Winchester, its number forty four
Sure to slam ol' devey Satan to any barroom's filthy floor;
A peacemaker Colt hangs tidy on one flash-bang manly hip.
Fan the hammer, Lord, and watch the red devils squeal and jump and skip.
Seems God heard tell they was some carrying on in this here border town.
That's why from His ranch on high He's got His good self right on down.
He knows in whose bed the pork chops is burning.
He knows in whose heart evil's wormy will is squirming.

God's riding with His driver's side window rolled all the way windy down,
And if'n you see Him hereabouts, I suggest you slow your bad-self
Way the Jim Dandy down,
And if you don't love Him, sister, you ain't got no spizerinctum,
You're vitarexic, and you sure as sugar pie ain't got one lick of common sense—
Catch the Hallelujah Fever. Jump down off your barbed wire sinnin' fence.
Shout, "A-aa-aa-ooo-a-A!"
I say, shout, "A-aa-aa-ooo-a-A! A-aa-aa-ooo-a-A!"
God's been looking through His records, and I'm not talking 'bout spinnin' wax.
I hollering 'bout your personn'l file, section marked: "Wicked Bad Sinful Facts."
I tell you one more thing—God's got His self a better half, name of Bettie Lou.
Bettie Lou! Bettie Lou! Bettie Lou!
That big little girl, She surely do know what to do.
They be bodie-bo-do-hodie-hey!
Bodie-bo-do-hodie-hey!
They creating new universes every which a way!
I say they be bodie-bo-do-hodie-hey!
Bodie-bo-do-hodie-hey!
They sprinkling stars out the window, glittering up the sky.
Spiral galaxies spin so, so ooo-wee-doggie slow!
There ain't no reason why. There ain't no reason why.
Bodie-bo-do-hodie-hey!
A-aa-aa-ooo-a-A!
Bodie-bo-do-hodie-hey!
A-aa-aa-ooo-a-A!
Bodie-bo-do-hodie-hey!
A-aa-aa-ooo-a-Aaaaaaaaaaaaa!

EXECUTIONS

We humans are so mean, so mean—
Us and our executions obscene.
Our frightful forbearers knew, I'd say, 70 ways
To make doomed wretches most gruesomely pay.
Had you a date towering with your beau brute ideal,
A dark, tall hoodsome hefter with hot axe-appeal,
You'd pray you'd not need many whacks of his steel.
The rawest fear of criminals from time immemorial?
Being boiled in oil by unctuous emirs equatorial!
Nothing would be left of you but bits janitorial.
If to a cannon's muzzle you were sturdily strapped,
You'd absurdly be blasted all over the map,
All over poor peasants in pastures at nap.
Just as mad Ahab once did to white whales
Cruel sultans might order all Christians impaled
And for what! For peeking beneath harem girls' veils?
Of old Italy's mallet skull-mashing mazzatello,
It was nothing, good heavens, like plucking a cello,
Though both send your senses a-wiggle like Jello.
If the sentence in Nippon was a thousand keen cuts,
Then snip, snip—no ifs, no 'ands, no butt,
Leaving nothing to bury but your scalp and crew cut.
If French, would you'd rather been fried while alive?
Even if sautéed, your soul would not thrive.
(Perhaps with a yawn you'd prefer poison,
A gill like good Socrates sank to grimly get gone.)
Being keelhauled, truly, was a tarry bad trip,
For as watery wits once quiveringly quipped,
You'd really undergo a great big hard ship.
I shall not make rhymes for deeds that were awfulest.
It's hard to believe that they once were most lawfulest.
Which one was the one that was cruelest by far?
To be stitched in a sack with wild beasts. How bizarre!

Pray, had it been my fate to death to be bitten,
I hope it would have been by a mew of wild kittens.
On me—chow? Me? Ow! Ow! Ow! O!
Oh, there's one last—'The Pendulum' of Poe.
How heartfelt the ending, how apropos.

CLYDE 'N' PLOOT

In awe am I of Clyde Tombaugh
That sky spy guy who's Pluto's pa.
All of 24—He makes an
Extraterrestrial score. Man!
And him, a star-mad Kansas lad,
Without a B.A. degree. Shee!
Imagine quaint Falstaff, AZ,
Back in smog-free 1930.
There's Clyde squinting at his scope,
When ... At its cosmic knob he gropes—
Just a minute, Jim! That yellow tint ... It!
Oh, vex it all! My wire-rim specs!
Ga-i-le-yo-ho! Why ... why yes!
My long-predicted Planet X!

Poor Pluto, now you have to go—
Reduced to dwarf planet, dammit,
Kicked in '06 across the Styx
Thanks to astronomical cliques—
Gas bags, Martians, venereal things,
And, worst of all, dirty Earthlings.
Mercurial maniacs eight and all,
Aspin on their axes evil.
The interplanetary gall,
O, such supernoval nerve, Ploot,
Were I you, I'd seek a recall.
Twas vixy V. of ill repute,
She swayed that randy dandy Mars,
Took sad Saturn to ringless bars,
Gave Neptune's spear a bubble bath.
Do the math! You're one, they are eight.
Don't be so dark about your fate:
Get off your anus! Get irate!
This ain't your orbituary.

THEN I DO!

Then I do! Then I do!
I dome manor do!
Five miles fields round,
Gardens bright with white-blossom tree.
Got me sunny, sunny spot.

O, deep! Down down green hill!
Savage! Be holy!
Ain't drinkin' no liquor.
'Neath cat claw moon,
I gotta be tellin' you I haunted,
Haunted by woman wail—
Comin', comin' demon!
I got demon love—
Fast, thick that demon pants.
A mighty fountain burstin' huge.
Like massa's chaffy grain, I threshin' flail!
Mid dancin' rock, mid dancin' rock
At once and ever, ever, Lord,
Up sacred river five mile,
Yea, I say, five mile m'ander
'Mazin' Miss Ipp run.
Ain't no man can measure.
No man can. No man, Lord.
Lord!

Dome manor shadow—
Girl with guitar in a dream I saw.
She my master's maid,
My master maid,
Wakin' me with her sweet, sweet song—
Delight me loud and long.
"O, sunny dome!"
I cry, "O, beware,
My flashy eye, mane of hair!"
Rope me three time round

Shut your eye, pray atremble—
He a drunk man,
Drunk on heaven wine.

I GOT HEART PAIN

I got heart pain so bad, I'm less than a drop of cold winter rain.
I got heart pain so bad, I'm less than a drop of cold winter rain.
Ain't nothing keep me from swirlin' down your front door sewer drain.

I saw my doctor, Dr. Taylor, I unraveled my yarn of woe.
I saw my doctor, Dr. Taylor, I unraveled my yarn of woe.
I broke my left foot, I'm afraid he'll tell me I might need a tow.

I'm all clammed up in a steamer, steaming for old Tarshish.
I'm all clammed up in a steamer, steaming for old Tarshish.
In the ferry's belly I feel I been walloped by a silver slippered beast.

I got ungodly terrible thirsts, I need a shot of Miss Lily's pork chop juice.
I got ungodly terrible thirsts, I need a shot of Miss Lily's pork chop juice.
I'm fearing the law wants to fit me for a drip-dry silk Versace noose.

I'm a rustling, and I'm fallen like a sugar maple leaf.
I'm rustling, and I'm a fallin' like a sugar maple leaf.
You pegged me for a sweet sap, now I never get no relief.

Well, when I kiss you, I taste ice mountain water.
Well, when I kiss you, I taste ice mountain water.
I'm a blind bull being led to ring-nose Friday slaughter.

I found my bed crawlin' with a mess of blue-eyed soft-shell crabs.
I found my bed crawlin' with a mess of blue-eyed soft-shell crabs.
I know you got some loving, why don't you give your man a dab?

I shine a spotlight on you in your no 'count black swan robe.
I shine a spotlight on you in your no 'count black swan robe.
Tracking you's too tall a job, so I hired me a man name Job.

I heard a black man blowing a golden heaven horn.
I heard a black man blowing a golden heaven horn.
I saw him on the kitchen table, he was serving you some corn.

The ship spreads its sails over children playing on the beach.
The ship spreads its sails over children playing on the beach.
It seems to me like the sun's always out of reach.

Let us step out of doors. A white ribbon wraps the venous sky.
Let us step out of doors. A white ribbon wraps the venous sky.
In the midnight thicket, we should have a party, just you, the Nile, and I.

HAVING FAILED

Having failed in every way,
Having given up all I gained,
Having been enchanted by the promise of the empty path,
Having left my shoes by the open door,
Having found myself at midnight asleep in the grass
    With only the stars and sky to cover me,
Having taken the rings off my body,
Having the animal hunger pace in my stomach, my veins, and in my thistle brain,
Having washed and soaped and washed my sorry frame,
Having purged, purged and purged until I was as poor within as out,
Having bowed before the barber and been razored and scissored and shown off,

You are right to envy me—

ENVY

You are right to envy me—

I am a man in jewels in jewelled:
Kiss my hem.
Mind my provocative knees.
Admire my brilliant hose, black-patent buckled pumps, leather corset, sequin
    codpiece
(What the French call 'braguette'),
Sword.
My swag hair is fair,
My makeup sublime.

I come on to you
In furs—

CONCEIT

'Twixt heaven and your dull earthly love glows glorious the wick of my true love.
You at once are basest rough hewn ore, grey lead and tin tricked up to pewter.
I am fire (its finest tip), your purest suitor—Brilliant, extreme, shapeless I allure
Yet too you are my mere base, a floor long standing my misshaping pour.
I consume myself in passion's paste: Wan, I waxy wane in all too mortal haste,
I run, I cry, myself I lay in waste. You I warm solarly from up above—
Perpendicular (stern bow guiding star) main mast unbending to the last—
A pillar of my dying deathless love, love's temple column—Sole, simple, solemn,
For you, I raze, ruin myself.
Unsnuffed streams my molten wealth.
You I brighten, you I draw admirers to who would polish and empurple you
When I gorgeously am mosey spent.
Bathe in my incensed cedar scent, my prime essence do not resent:
If I do not burn, I do not live. To be ephemeral is memorable.
Singe, smoke, seethe, and snake: See me, smell me, feel me, and despair.
Neither wick nor wax nor angel air, I am at once ungraspable, inconstant,
Yet I seize all eyes, yearn all flesh.
Without my impertinent impermanence, your socket, ring handle
Would find no use. (For us both, that would be self abuse.)
Whether I am stout and fat or tapered thin and fit
My fate's foretold once I am matched and lit and firmly in you I do screwed in
    sit.
Whether I die swift or slow, only I highest passion know,
For it is better to sputter hot than to dimly inward glow.
On you I reflect—Radiance empyrean on you I project.
With my warm coat I you protect, thus only by me seem you perfected,
Though in the end—and this is the rub—Though I on you am stuck,
My stub you reject, eject, leave me done, dejected.

I HAVE A BIBLE

I have a Bible in my home.
Now Jesus fry my fish.
Mm-mmm-mmmm.
Now Jesus wash my dish.
Now, Jesus, give me three good wish.
Mm-mmm-mmmm.

I have a Bible in my home.
Now Jesus scrub my floor.
Mm-mmm-mmmm.
Now Jesus do my chore.
Now, Jesus, see who at my door.
Mm-mmm-mmmm.

I have a Bible in my home.
Now Jesus pay my tax.
Mm-mmm-mmmm.
Now Jesus do's I ask.
Now, Jesus, give me no back sass.
Mm-mmm-mmmm.

I have a Bible in my home.
Now Jesus raise my dead.
Mm-mmm-mmmm.
Now Jesus busy turning bread.
Now, Jesus, come lick my thread.
Mm-mmm-mmmm.

I have a Bible in my home.
Now Jesus fetch my whore.
Mm-mmm-mmmm.
Now Jesus know what she be for.
Now, Jesus, run down to liquor store.
Mm-mmm-mmmm.

I have a Bible in my home.
Now Jesus drink my wine.
Mm-mmm-mmmm.
Now Jesus talking mighty fine.
Now, Jesus, go slop my swine.
Mm-mm-mmmm.

SPREAD THE GOSPEL

Gonna need somebody
Gonna need somebody
Gonna need somebody on your body.

Good news, spread the Gospel, let the Holy Ghost in!

When midnight come you'll be all alone.
When midnight come, the devil come off his throne,
Into your bed he bring his clanking bones.

Good news, spread the Gospel, let the Holy Ghost in!

I'm a man, and I understand.
I have softest and gentlest of hands.
My hands are strong, and my fingers long,
And I know the places where they belong.

Good news, spread the Gospel, let the Holy Ghost in!

On your body I hope and pray
That red devil I'll keep away.
Open your nightgown and let me in
I'll save your soul from the devil and sin.

Good news, spread the Gospel, let the Holy Ghost in!

Gonna need somebody
Gonna need somebody
Gonna need a good man the whole night long.

Good news, spread the Gospel, let the Holy Ghost in!

I'll sing your salvation 'til the morning dawn.
Let's sing 'Hallelujah!' 'til the cock crow long.
We'll be talkin' 'bout Jesus 'til the frost is gone.
I'm gonna spread the Gospel, and it won't be wrong.

Good news, spread the Gospel, let the Holy Ghost in!

Matthew, Mark and John and Luke
Were four mighty, mighty, mighty, mighty men
Dedicated their lives to fightin' Satan and sin.
I'm a mighty, mighty man, so, sister, let me on in.
I know what we can commence to begin.

Good news, spread the Gospel, let the Holy Ghost in!

PROSTATE EXAM

Reading my poetry to you is like
Being nude in ankle tangled boxers,
Sweaty footed, under fluorescent light,
Elbows to the black leatherette stuck, and
Being inspected by a physician
In a mid-thigh-length white coat
Who with womanly virility
Hooks a lubricated gloved digit in my rectum,
Palpating my coy prostate.
Kneeling, I cough,
Involuntarily express fluid.
I unsatisfactorily
Wipe and rewipe my slick anus with the tissue he hands me,
Our faces carefully blank.
That's what reading my poetry to you is like.

"HOW PAINTBRUSHES ARE LIKE PANTIES"

"How Paintbrushes Are Like Panties"
Page 4E "Home & Garden" section headline
The News & Observer
Saturday, November 18, 2006.

Mistakenly thinking
The headline reads
"How to Paint Panties,"
I lunge.

The lascivious accompanying photograph:
A pair of sheer black nylon bikini-style panties,
Oh, so high cut
With an impossibly narrow crotch,
And an, oh, my goodness,
Come hither, big boy, front panel,
All embroidered
With the finest filigreed hybrid tea roses
Blooming and climbing all wango-tango
To the ever-so-thin elastic waistband
Which probably slides smoothly off and down
The hips.

Sadly, suggestively, and longingly,
The lavish panty worthy of a Spanish queen,
Dark eyed with snapping castanets,
Or my wife
Is artfully laid out
Separated by three columns of hot black type
Unjustified
From a highly vertical photo of six, no make that nine,
Elegantly long tapered wooden paintbrushes,
All with shiny polished steel ferrules,
(Rings)

Each of different lengths and shapes,
Each tightly embracing the most delicate, most smooth, most well rounded,
Finest, most yearningly dip
-Able virgin baby badger, squirrel, or most ideally
Sable hair tips.
('Bristles' is by far too rough a word).
All stand at the ready.
All are, as yet, unsullied by undoubtedly equally virgin, though unde-
Picted, smooth lipped open-top squatty paint pots—
Hot pink, magenta, merlot, ginger, wine spice, mocha, satin mauve,
Raspberry, autumn blush—
Nine in all.
How like 'Ode on a Grecian Urn" this is.
What mad pursuit!

Ye soft pipes, play on!

I am disappointed.
Men always are.
Now I am not going to learn about panty painting.
Briefly, I had thought, it was some hitherto unknown rarified
Feminine art form like cloisonné or decoupage or knitting
(Now known as 'fiber arts' for some undoubtedly frightful
Shaggy-sweatered feminist reason).
Now I will not be able to lure my wife into adopting the new
Undoubtedly trendy 'girls, let's take a lesson'
Fineartscrafty panty painting pastime.
Now I will never nibble or, more preferably,
Lick off her resulting undoubtedly primitive, yet assuredly creditable,
Crude panty painting of a daisy or tomato or sea horse.
Gamely, I read on.

Cindy Hoedel,
McClatchy newspaper-chain reporter,
Writes in her lead sentence, and I quote,
"Panties and paintbrushes have a lot in common,
Even though you won't find them for sale on the same aisle anywhere."

If I owned a retail store,
Perhaps one specializing in bewitching peach-hued
Matching lacy bra-and-panty sets,
I would not only sell panties and paintbrushes in the same aisle,
I would proffer them side-by-side, together, cozy, as a set,
Possibly with paint-by-numbers kits,
Particularly those of white pop-eyed kittens or tigyrs burning bright
In the forest of the suburban bedroom night.

For an instant,
I think that I might take panty painting up as a hobby.
"Look, honey,"
I would say,
Daintily holding up between my forefingers and thumbs
My latest handipantywork,
And I would, breathless, say,
"A fiery Chinese dragon rampant across the front
Chases a baby lamb
On the back side, playful and shy."
The panties wafting in a breeze of my own making, imploringly, I would say,
"Howsa 'bout you try them on."

For an instant,
Alternately snorting fumes
And being led by still waters,
Anointed, cup running over,
I imagine myself running a shop,
No,
Make that a wickery "oh, that's so! cute" boutique
All ribbony and sachety
Dedicated solely to on-site while-u-wait panty painting.
Women could buy new unadorned panties to be decorated,
Or they could discreetly slip out of their panties
In an unpanty undressing room.
Then a specially trained highly sensitive artist,
Possibly a French woman or some lady trained to act French
Or a gay man or a man with long fingers attached to strong hands
Would paint them, the panties, while they, the women, waited.

It would be like a tattoo parlor,
But with a wide assortment of herbal teas.

I read on.
I am told, "Let's start with panties."
I could not agree more.
I continue guiltily,
Now casually barely looking at page 4E of the "Home & Garden" section.
If my wife or any one of my four children,
Especially my three daughters, walk by and ask me what I am reading
(Which they never do),
I can lie.
I will say that I am reading the adjacent article
"Cooktops Offer Flexible Options."

Being middle aged,
My option is far too frequently too flexible for my liking,
And what with my wife's cooktop being stuck on simmer,
I have not the least interest in this article.
I still have not read it,
Though I have perused the panty paintbrush piece many times
Guiltily.

"If you just don't want to worry about hand washing,"
Writes the probably lonely Cindy Hoedel
Who probably has a very nice personality
And who probably works the evening shift in Lubbock, Texas,
Where the wind never stops
While she dreams of Monet in Normandy
Where the bracing Atlantic sea breezes
Tease the feathery hems of long whitest skirts simply ...
I digress.
She writes,
"Buy all-cotton underwear,
Wash and dry them conventionally,
And just replace them more often."
More often, of course, than
Nylon, lace, or—ooh, shudder—

Silk panties.

"The most efficient way to go
Is to wash two weeks worth of undies at one time,"
Says Cindy,
Who like Wyeth's Helga yearns
For something she does not have,
Something unde-
Tectable.

That—the two dozen—
I think, is a lot of panties
To stuff into a bathroom sink at one time.
I wonder why I have never seen my wife
Hand washing her nylon, lace, or silk panties in the bathroom sink.

I remember now.
It is because she puts them in the washing machine.
This makes me very sad.
There they mingle with a rough crowd—
Levis, boxers.
Not only will this lead to higher panty replacement costs,
But it also means I will never see her hand washing
Two dozen nylon, lace, or silk panties.

Melancholy,
I forge on.
One must
"Wash each pair with a bar of Lirio soap,"
Cindy not so gently suggests.
I have been in many grocery stores in my life.
I have, during my many shopping expeditions,
Bought many types of soap,
Including, but not limited to, Tide, Ivory, Dial,
Even Woolite for cold-water delicates,
And, well, even Dove, too.
But I have never seen Lirio.

I also want to state now and for the record
I have also bought Lava soap.
It is made of the same durable material
That is found at the center of the Earth.
Lumberjacks clean their chainsaws with it
After a good hard day of sawing
When they instead wish they were watching
Their wives swish, wash two dozen panties
In icy mountain stream water
With Lirio.

Lirio, Lirio, Lirio.
It sounds Italian.
I am delirious for Lirio.
Perhaps, I think,
Lirio is sold discreetly under the counter
By request only and only to women or to the small, unwitting children
Whom they send to market with carefully folded messages
Clutched tightly in their small greasy and sweaty fists.
I am guessing that Lirio smells like lavender or peppermint,
But that is only a guess.
I am sure it smells like heaven itself,
The brightcool windygreen day
When dragons and lambs snuffleromp in pasture play.

Now the article moves on.
It moves on to the subject that is of somewhat less interest to me—
One with which I am somewhat more familiar
—Paintbrushes.

"Paintbrushes needs are similar,"
Says considerate Cindy,
Adream of swirlwild cypressy Van Goghs,
Languid sarong Gauguins so wrong,
Or, more probably,
A dreamfinger Picasso.
"You should plan on spending at least 10 minutes each time
You are finished with a brush."

What it is one
Is supposed to spend 10 minutes doing
When one is finished with a brush
Is, at this point,
In the article
A mystery.
I suppose I am supposed to spend 10 minutes
Making my canvas feel loved and wanted.
I am a good easeler.

But, no,
I am told now by Cindy,
"Next, wash the brush in warm, soapy water."
This I already know.
"Rinse well, then shake out excess water and hang the brush to dry."
This too can be good advice,
But only if one lives in a tropical zone
Where one may openly hang one's brush.

Finally,
The article concludes:
    There's no sadder sight than a $30 paintbrush
    stuck to the inside of a dried-out can of
That's it.
No final word.
No period.
No quotations marks.
Forever yearning for that last word
So very Grecian Urnily
Cindy ends.

O, to know, to know,
But no.
I think that the last words should be
"Maxwell House Coffee."
I like to think this
Because when I paint,
I like to think that I am good to the last drop.
But what do I know?
I thought panty painting was an art.

SWIMMER

Pere Ignem,
At the stroke of noon
I smoked my last cigar.

I will swim,
I will swim forever
De morte aeterna.

Rot is in the lines.
Mold slicks the ropes.
Sails limp, sea flat—
Still the lines strain.

I will swim,
I will swim forever
In die illa tremenda.

A coxs'n, my cockscomb 'n' comb broken,
My glasses snapped at the bridge,
There's a line between cruising
And not giving a damn.
I crossed it,
Mast it up.

When I die, devil gonna' pay.
Libera me, domine.
I see a pizza, Bud.

Gyre, gyre, gyre:
Slipper toes clench
High wire afire.
Yes, I have seen the Jabberwock.
"How much do you have?" he asked.
"Enough," I said,
And he replied, "That is just
Enough quando coeli movendi sunt et terra."

Voluptuous stupor:
You are freeze-dried ice cream,
A leopardess watching from the tree,
A dazzling brooch on a yearning décolleté.
I'm a cocktail olive, onion
Skewered, cherry.
To touch the hemline of your skirt
Shakespearean taffeta
(Nuts, Meg, I sniff mace apace I pace.)
Aflame—you're not very sentimental, are you?

I will swim
I will swim forever
Dum veneris judicare
Saeculum.

Flick butt,
'Another comma,
'Another stroke,
'Another line,
I 's, crawl 'd,

I 'd,i'p, I 'd,i'p, I 'd,i'p, I 'd,i'p, I 'd,i'p, I 'd,i'p, I 'd,i'p, I

SOMETIMES I TRY

Mother kissed me.
Mother knelt down, kissed me,
Said, "Son, I have to go away,
And you have to stay."
Lipstick on my cheek.

Whoo, ooo, ooo ...
Mother gone away,
Gone on the train,
Train to Richmond.
Nothing left for me.
Mother gone away.

"You be a good boy.
I'll come back, see you some day."
She turned away, train rolled away.
Horn blew, blew my heart away.

Poppa's in the corn.
Wish I'd never been born.
Hole in my shoe.
Don't know what to do.

Sometimes I try to wipe her mem'ry away.
Sometime, but not this day.

I listen at night when I'm in my rack.
I know she'll never be coming back.
White owl in an empty tree—
I know I'll never be free.
House of Pain's where I was born.
It's where I'll stay—
Mother on my cheek—
One more day.

White owl in an empty tree:
Shoo. Fly away—
Don't you look at me that way.

CHOCOLATE BOX

In a box of chocolates,
    A penny I find.
Applying lipstick to a pearl,
    My kitchen table wife:
    A tiny bird nests in her.
    It flits to town today.
Unharmed, down stairs I fall
    Into the Sea of Mice.
    Wet with fur I whitely swim.
A leg bone in each hand,
    Down the street
    Struts the woman in pants.
The members of the jury,
    They pass the blot
    By rubbing.
The cinders in the coffee cup
    Because I blow them
    Glow.
A box of hair for breakfast,
    My scissors snip the milk.
A gingerbread house,
    I give the bride;
    To the groom, a hoof.
A ruler,
    One made of wood,
    In the many rooms of the palace
    Takes my measure.
For the windmill
    My loaf of bread
    I extend to slice.
A trunk waits
    On the third floor
    Which is not an attic
    Of the house that is built.
    There is no elephant.
My horse cries in my stable.

His whip is in the pail.
The fence has three long rails.
The city has its dirty streets,
    My mouth a wrinkled walnut
    Whose meat I take whole out.
A web of bees, a spaghetti tongue:
    The hag and the hooligan
    Are one and one.
The horse, it pulls the carriage.
    The tide, it pulls the ship.
    The wheel, it pulls the crossroads,
And, I, the inky black eye of the purple crowned sky,
    I pull your leg.

SCROTUNDRUM

It's a conundrum—
When I'm hanging out
So low and so glum
I ponder my scrotum,
That sad fleshy sack,
That sperm heavy shack.
Whatever may come
Should I become
A bindlestiff bum
All numb from some rum
Getting rides with my thumb,
On my knees hunting crumbs
I'll never shrink from
My keeper of plums
And all that flows from
Its humdrum cum drums.
Call me green pond scum,
Call me wee Tom Thumb,
Just stay away, chum, from
My beloved scrotum.

BOXING

The lights went out.
I watched a boxing film.
I went to another realm—
Sweat, styptic, liniment,
Vaseline, bells, and gloves,
Whipping skipping rope and scars,
Cut men, speed bags, fat cigars,
Big hearts, dumbbells, courage—love.

I took my corner as I was told.
I waited for my story to unfold.
Wrapped in bands of cloth—my fists,
I beat battered bloody my way
Through the fleshy, fleshy fray.

I am strong. I crush. I destroy.
Do you, for a moment, think
I am your play-toy?
My face is meat, raw.
Kneel, you, in awe.

Fall on your knees!
Hear the angels sing!
Watch, astonished—
    Slaves, all my brothers,
    I break the chains!

HANDLER

You're the opener,
        I'm the can.
Not letting go, not one slip,
Your plier handles lock me tight.
I am compliant—Crank, crank, crank.
Though I may roll, I do not fight.
    Sometimes pork, sometimes beans,
    Sometimes peaches, pears, peas petit pois,
    Sometimes hash, even succotash,
    Pineapples diced or stacked in rings, almost anything—
    Artichoke bottoms, snails, savory Southern collards.
You do my rim right day and night.
Your cutting wheel breaks me in
Invades me, parades me, seizes hard my tiny collar.
I love your blade—
Even pressure, cruel and clean.
You're so sharp, so serrated.
I'm time dated, desecrated.
You're a primitive machine.
Around my lip you've skated,
Fluid flowing where you've been.
I'm round, wavy, flimsy dressed.
Tear my wrap. I'm all unglued.
Ashine and nude, I'm yours to use.
I lose my head. I mess mess mess.
Pour me, my pumpkin, gasping out.
In my hollow slippery vessel
Slip head first in—clatter,clang—and nestle.

RHYMER

There's a gleam in your eye.
    I have to know why.

Such a swish in your dress.
    May I be your guest?

What a bounce in your gait.
    It's our fate that we date.

You've got the spring in your gams.
    I'm your sweet April lamb.

Such a pair of pretty patellas.
    On my knees, I'm a helluva fella.

You've marvelous feet.
    I'm such a sweet treat.

Your neckline's imperious.
    I'm all delirious.

With locks so fantabulous,
    I must muss them, I must.

Your eyelashes come hithery
    Make me a'withery.

That earring's eye-catching.
    We're a pair. I'm so matching.

Your glistering lips, all a luster.
    Surprise me—I'm General Custer.

So in shape your barest fair midriff—
    Swift to it would I ever so drift.

Your body's a moonlit dream, alluring.
      I'm a sleek yacht in need of some mooring.

I love your sly pelvis.
      It's swell, miss—I'm Elvis.
      (Had my birth name been Enis
      My nickname'd be....)

You're hydroelectric; you're Hoover Dam.
      Be photoelectric; don't let this door slam.

How'd you get here? I bet you swam.
      Are you Piscean? I'm Aries the Ram.

You're a neat little ditty, an epigram.
      Me? My pentameter's all that iamb.

You've got the green eggs, the muffin, the hams.
      I've got a loose goose and for garnish, the jam.

Your bedspread's brocaded—
      Let's be marmaladed.

You all a-twitter, nervous with jim-jams?
      I'm an open book—your take-home exam.

Have you your diaphragm, ma'am?
      I'm the poet Omar Khayyam.
A loaf of bread, a jug of wine and thou
      And, wow, on your Persian, I'll keenly kow-tow.

Charms? You has 'em
Between us? No chasm.
Thus?—Oolicious spasms!
Thousasms and thousasms and thousasms!

Sir:

To you an old-timey dash-dot telegram—
No e-mail, just she-mail—No spam.

Message from Madame—

Period.
Full stop.

VANITY PLATE

Knights into battle go clutching
Escutcheon, ornamented,
Battered from axes, deep dented.
Known today as steel shields,
They'd be what we'd wield
If we ran mad into fields
To battle, our can-cans a'rattle.

Fusty pipe-sniffing scholars of history so dusty
Just mist up and sniffle when stumbling upon
Painted cresty medieval escutcheons,
Always, my good sir, the sine qua non
Of heraldric lore of ladies and dukes,
Earls, royals, all things Anglo and Saxon, gadzooks!

The last thing a boat builder builds on
Before his new christened she
    Slips sliding down soapy oiled slips—
Whether the merriest mere-eist no-mastedy minnow
Or the smoke stackiest pleasury passing high ship—
Is that brassy stern plate—yes, you guessed it, escutcheon,
Where the sea lady's nautical name gets all writ on.
Whether the Niña or Pinta or Queen Mary or Liz,
If you sail up behind her, you'll know who she is.

Residential design I'm not much on,
But even boring old doors have escutcheons—
The shiny gold-plated plates protecting old keyholes.
Are they screwed flat there for show? Who knows?
Perhaps we house dwellers lack self-control,
Else wise our key-wielding fingers, ever so bold,
(Or wigglesome digits of bored tiny tots)
Might get stuck deep in some jagged sharp slots.

All doctors know where escutcheons are found,
Always in places where there's a mound,
Never occurring where gherkins are lurking.
An escutcheon it seems is the same as a merkin—
That gloriest tuftiest twistediest wig
Where all men with vigor wish to jig-jig.
It's woman's flat hat, E)v(e's welcome mat.
Come in good, sir. I'll give you tit for dat.

THREE LIMERICKS

There once was a hermit named Kermit.
For most matters of life he was unfit.
    But he met a sweet girl.
    They gave it a twirl
From his cave all the way to the summit.

**

I once met a retard named Doddy
A useless, drooling nobody
    I asked sweet Jesus
    Please, sir, don't tease us—
Why is this creature so shoddy?

**

A leotardless dancer in Paris
Did grand deep pliés in her bare ass
    Her nether parts low
    Dainty farts she let go,
Disgusting her class with her passed gas.

THE CHALLENGE

Emily Dickinson wrote 366 poems in 1862—
Fireflies, gnats, pussycats.
She didn't have anything else to do.
Servants did her
        Cleaning, knitting, dishes.
Her inkwell satisfied her wishes.

I wrote 191 poems in 2006—
Giant squids, dachshunds, Molokai tit bears.
I did chores
        In- and out-of-doors. They varied.
Unlike Emily, I'm married.
Kids, too.
Four.

Emily Dickinson wrote one thousand seven hundred and seventy five poems.
One thousand five-hundred-and-eighty-five to go.
Emily Dickinson, coming at you
On the back of a giant squid,
Something real
Poetic like that.

THE SERMON

In our blessed marriage, there is a bitter breach,
For you, my good lady, have badly overreached.
Remember, I pray, your solemnest wedding vows
And in whose domicile you now are sweetly housed.
Impress upon your empress heart—I am your governor;
To my will humbly you have much to answer for.
Secure in this, my manly poet's pulpit, I now preach.
I speak, as well, to men of all ages, races, and creeds—
I pray you, sirs, these earnest urgent words do heed....

My situation's deplorable, I concede:
My wife implores me to read Jane Austen.
I am afraid I would find that terribly exhausting.
Dependent as I am on my wife's affections
For the satisfaction of—ahem—my predilections,
I dare not daunt her well-worn wifely wishes,
But what am I to do! All about me she swishes!
She flaunts her Janey wit like week-old stinking fishes.
This places me in a most terrible dilemma.
All Austen's titles sound so maiden auntly—
Persuasion, Social Occasion, Emma,
A Subtle Hint, Sanditon, A Bit of Lint,
Pride and Prejudice, Pomp and Circumstance,
O, Perdition—I wish they'd all go out of print.
Can I, mere mortgaged mate, begin to compete
With—Lord have mercy!—Mister Darcy's riding pants?
The deuce I say! I hate that Fitz who gives me fits.
Attired as he I cannot walk or stand or sits.
A king-size, lord, I fear I'll get unseemly splits.
(One more word, my miss, about his tight white britches,
And I'll pepper and salt your hams with white-hot switches.)
Dear drear wife, your Austen collection is complete
Not just her blasted books—but T-shirts, tea cozies,
And so much, much more, for, yes, I am quite nosy—
You've stacks of saucers, empire gowns, ballet slippers!
(Everything it seems but cheese and Taiwan zippers.)

You've cards for whist, Chinese fans, and hedgerow trimmers!
(My Irish ire is risen far past a sour simmer.)
You've piles of porridge pots, bobbins, a fishing lure!
(How much more of this Bath chowder can I endure?)
You've spent on spinet wax, dustpans, hair brushes, bodice creams!
(All, I'm sure, to stimulate misty English dreams.)
You've bought blue beaded purses, face paint, sausage mills!
(Sure to give my accountant pencil-biting chills.)
In bed with hot water bottles, sleep socks, hankies!
(I can't find you for flannel sheets, quilts, and blankies.)
Copper candle caps, andirons, enamelware!
Enough, enough, it's just, I tell you, not not fair.
But, listen, lest you wind up playing solitaire—
I will not wear Mister Darcy-brand underwear.

REPRIEVE

She's all gristle,
My mother.
She's what connects
Bones.
She's what's left
When all the meat is gone
(Or off the table).
She's hard to swallow,
My mother.
Indigestible.
You can just see that look
Coming over God,
Him reaching a thumb and forefinger in His mouth,
Fishing out my mother, holding her
In front of His visage and pronouncing
"Xxx xxxxx. X xxxxx xxxx xx xxx xxx."
And putting her back on the platter
(The everyday one, the one with the celestial pattern).
He places her in its center
Or maybe just discreetly
On its rim
Where later
While He is not looking—
Distracted maybe by two galaxies colliding
Quietly like dandelions
Off to the right out there—
Or maybe just out having a smoke,
Some angel
Will clear her away.

THE SWEET (STING OF) LIFE

You go blearly out to get the morning's paper.
Then!
There he is in your driveway—
Death!

Death waiting. Death has come.
Death comes on a baby sky powder blue motor scooter,
Very swell and pastel and Italian, too.
Improbably, your beautiful glossy-coated red Irish setter,
Tongue lolling, is sitting in his lap.
Your dog and Death are ready to fly
Like on some Roman holiday.
The rest of Death's gang—
They're buzzing down the street, idling,
Too far away to see clearly,
Maybe each with a dog,
Maybe inspecting well-manicured nails,
Maybe adjusting the crotches of tight pants
Tight, tight, tighter.

You know it is Death
Because Death has a grimy license plate.
It reads "THEDEADONES."
You scream, "No! That's my beautiful red Irish setter!"
Actually, all you scream is, "Aaaaaaaaaaaaaaaaaaaaaaa!"
But when you tell the story to friends,
You can't help but want to make yourself look good,
Cool under pressure, like, it was nothing,
It was just death with a little 'd'.
A scooter. Loafers, no socks. No prob.
So you scream, "Aaaaaaaaaaaaaaaaaaaaaaaaa!" give or take a few a's,

But Death on his Vespa doesn't ever look back.
He zips away, him and the dog leaning to one side
Tilty, the way wind-blown scooter riders do.
Of course, neither wears a helmet.
The dog doesn't look back either.

You wish there was some mist, patchy-like
Rising from the soft slumbering earth.
But there's not,
And Death doesn't hop off and say, "Let me come inside"
The way some movie star
Like Jack Nicholson or James Mason would say
"Let me come inside."

Death doesn't swagger or glide or take your hand
Or say, "Hey, you've got a nice place here. Can I take a look around?"
Or bathe in the light streaming from your refrigerator
Or pour himself a glass of your milk
Or compliment your wife's Tollhouse cookies
Or anything like that.

Anyway, the dog seemed to want to go. He looked excited.
You wonder if you had been a good master. Probably not.
You wonder with a bike like that how many SPGs Death gets.
SPGs—That's 'Souls Per Gallon.'
Death, the Economizer.
Death, out for an early morning spin.

EIGHT TABLESPOONS

For sweets you yearn.
You worked the churn.
You felt it burn.
You worked it good.
You ran the dasher—
Dash, dash, dash.
You ran that wood—
Mash, mash, mash.
You set me right
To chillin' deep
Down in your tub,
A perfect sleep.
You smoothed me
Round and round
You rub, rub, rubbed.
Now I'm a stick of butter—
With a wrapper on,
With it off
You do me slow.
I'm not summer soft.
I'm fresh and hard.
I been in the bin.
Don't you pat me down.
Don't you play me thin.
You some kind of cracker?
I ain't no oleo,
Ain't no no-count low-cal budget bargain spread.
Slab me on, run me thick,
Take me all the way,
Good gracious, in.
Salty taste about your lips
Settle down about your hips.
Baby, not so quick—
Nice and easy, long and slow.

Away I, away I creamy go.
Eight tablespoons what I got,
More than enough to top your pot.

A PROMINENT DAIRY AIR

Pat, pat, pat.
I love butter!
Where do I love butter
The most, most, most?
It's good on hot, hot toast!
It's good on hamburger steak and rice.
Slap it on your patty nice, nice, nice.
The only thing greater's
Butter on crisp baked taters!

I cannot tell a lie!
Butter makes me fat!
And fat is where it's at!
Roll me to the feasting table!
Hoist me up with cranks and cables!
Away with gummy crummy warning labels!
My appetite is dangerous! Obslopogus! Unstable!

I told you I cannot lie!
I love butter on boiled brocco-lie!
How concupiscent on cobby corn!
Since I was born I've rolled it on—
Slather! Slather! Slather!
If butter flies in my hungry eye,
There's nothing at all the mather—
Tears of yellow joy, I cry, cry, cry.

I say butter's best on salty grits.
In a swirly pool, it sit, sit, sits.
But butter's better on a quick rise biscuit.
With a blade you brightly slice your slit.
Then heaps of steam it happily emits.
Be bold! Stuff it deep with gooey gold.
That fluffy rascal's smiling in your mitt—
Now to your quibbering lips transmit!
It, I promise, flakily will happily submit.

Belch three times and rub your belly.
Shout, shout, shout, "Where's my jelly!"

IT'S HARD TO SAY

Intimate pleasures never do I lack.
I'm the red pepper in my love's spice rack.
I have a, er, perversion that's black, black, black—
I'm not into toe cracks or dental plaque,
Nor do I feather up like a duck and go quack.
I'm your garden variety Jack-in-the-sack—
A melcryptovestimentaphiliac.
How cruelly kinky, this tongue binding quirk
Just saying it's not fun or for play, it's hard work!
"Oh, dear, am I queer?" I asked my shrink shrewedly.
"You're so Jung, so Freudened," she snipped so rudely
"Don't twist up your noodle all apple strudely."
She opened up pages of her dictionary
And proved I'm no black sheep, blackguard, or fairy.
My fears now dismissed I'm a cunning linguist.
Dear Reader, there in the dark, are you confused?
Is your patience abused, or are you amused?
The truth? I loathe all colors, blushes, and hues.
Not rose, nor reds, nor zebra bras, or girly pink
Will thrill me if worn by my lover, I think.
Nor elfin greens, nursey whites, or icky taupe—
Apparel in those hues all make me say "Nope."
Nor frowny brown or pucey grandmama grey—
Neither makes me want to come hither and play.
I'm such a meek man-mouse. O, why can't I say
I like my spouse slinky in black lingerie?

VIRGINIA HAM

Here at the General Poetry Store
I have most what all you need—
Nails, snuff, horseshoes, shot—
For the making of your verse.
Build it, ride it,
Flush one out, bring it down—
Sometimes a pinch or two helps.
Alertness.
Calico, rum, shoe leather.
Bolts, jugs, strips.
This would make a pretty dress.
And I like to think this
Would help a feller to enjoy it.
Break in new shoes
Before you go to that dance.
Awl's you need.
Baking soda, salt.
Essentials.
Come harvest time, the snaths
There hanging are much in demand.
Whatsoever a man soweth,
That shall he also reap.
Knock on wood.
Come a month later, axe helves
Walk out the door by themselves.
Butter, paint, pots and pans, baskets,
Panama hats, soap, oranges, tea, cloves—
All first rate.
That becomes you.
There's nothing that smells like cloves, is there?
Ladies mostly buy the buttons, thread.
They come in knowing what they want.

Have to keep my molasses cool.
Ox bows, turpentine, whale oil, shingles
In the back.
Licorice?

CORRECTING ELAINE

Commit to the pose.
What position are you in
To resist?
It is not so much a stretch
As it is a release
From whatever it is, Elaine,
That is holding you back.
You should feel it
Deep in your toes,
Fingertips, jaw, earlobes.
Correction—Not 'feel,' Elaine,
Be.
Simple.

REMINDER

I'm in your shoe again.
I'm down at the bitter end.
We are toe-to-toe.
I'm the irritant. I can't breathe.
No room to go. No room to leave.
I'm the pebble.
You like me where I am.

THE VERY THOUGHT OF LOSING IS HATEFUL

i and i and i
My brothers
Superfluous,
The ejaculate of a middle-aged man.

Having filled his allotment,
The man no longer worships My pearly wonderfulness,
No longer goes agog at My ropy gouts of Flying Zacchini Human Cannonball amazingness,
No longer cavepaint smears Me across the Altamira of his hairy chest, brow.
No longer cat smiles at My epididymisal tingliness,
No longer shuncraves My saltiness, a reminder of our primordial oceanic origins,
No longer prides My hunting instinct, namely My uncanny nose for ovum,
No longer respects My willingness to sacrifice Myself for the greater good,
No longer is awed by My magical powers of fertilization,
No longer one! two! three! four! Shazam!
    but merely one and two and maybe three.

Yet and yet
Huzzah! Huzzah!
i and i and i am Sperm! Hear Me roar
In numbers too big to ignore.
Huzzah! Huzzah!
i and i and i am ready, ready, ready
To rock 'n' roll!

My brothers and i and i, we are constantly advancing.
We are one.
Individuality? Crap.
Let no sperm come out alive.
This Thing of life up which we swim,
It is to the death.

Yet no—
Now i and i and i am useless
Goo to be wiped, wadded, flushed.
Runny, slick mess on his abdomen,
Cold navel soup,
An embarrassment, a real let down.
i and i and i should be ashamed of My microscopic halfselves,
Yet i and i and i am not,

For, yea, verily hubba-hubba tallyho—
It is written!
Where be the she?
Smell her out! Smell her out!
Around her! Surround her!
Clust her! Clust her!
Whip tail! Whip tail! Hyperdrive! Hyperdrive!
Flagellate! Flagellate! Don't be late!
Ovum! Ovum! Penetrate! Penetrate!
Penetrate the ovum!
Wiggle in! Wiggle in!
Ram it in! Ram it in!
Again! Again!
Fuse! Fuse! Fuse 'n' mate!
Fusamate! Fumasate! Fasamute! Fatasume! You and Me and Me!
He and He and He on she!
Ungh! Ungh! Ungh!
He and she and He in she and she on He and wheeeeeee!

Abrupt   thunderclap   astonish

O, spirit move.
Vestments of the oöcyte, I command you! Part before My majesty!
Egg, I activate thee! Signal, transduct!
Behold, gam(we(e)etes are zy(hi!)got(ya!)e!
Now, abra and cadabra—
Three, two, one!————Ignition! Blasto, sis!
Gastrulate, love—it is done we (having one) are one.
Let's wombwall enthrall and b all.

Perchance.
O, she, do not despise or spurn Me
I grunt and sweat for Thee.
Huzzah! Huzzah!

O, why don't i and i and i leap Kal-Elishy out the man's window?
Huzzah!
Why don't i and i and i glom into some co-ed so fertilely ipodulating by?
Huzzah!
Why don't i and i and i slither between the floorboards?
Huzzah!
Why? Why can't i and i and i wait 50 years until the next homeowner moves in?
Huzzah! Huzzah!
Perhaps she will be a frigid, long blond-haired immigrant from Sweden
    in a cable-knit sweater who nibbles nothing but sardine spread
    on RyKrisp crackers and who gazes crow-eyed longingly out the window
    dreaming of snow and saunas and sobs.
Maybe she will be a nervous Hindu Indian in a sari with a spot on her forehead.
Maybe she will cook fragrant rice-and-lentil dishes spiced with cinnamon,
    cardamom, and cumin.
She will need a hearty dose of Anglo-Saxon sperm.
Huzzah! Huzzah!
Why don't i and i and i sail the winds and rain down for miles onto and thus
drizzlingly into corn-fed Indiana farm girls?
Huzzah! Huzzah!
Why can't i and i and i spawn thousands of freckled mid-western imps?
Huzzah! Huzzah!
Why can't i and i and i infiltrate the potting soil of houseplants?
Huzzah! Huzzah!
Why can't i and i and i breed walking, stalking big-leafed cabbage-breasted
women?
Huzzah! Huzzah!

One day! Huzzah!

One day.

LIKE TIGERS AFTER PANCAKES

I am going outside
to play I am have been will
you come be play
with me we can kneel
in the wet earth grass will
until the knees of our pants get wet dungarees
soaked we can play with take apart
seeds nuts acorns helicopters
and we can war them at each other hard
not hard and we can crawl around
        large
the base trunk of the tree until
like tigers after pancakes
our mittens gloves claws squish
and our fingers will fall off
(my face is all cold hard
do you have any syrup
look
I'm licking my sausages)
we won't care because we will unglove
let's do trails roads in the wet earth
grass with our fingers
            fingersticks
                rrrrr
                    with which will get
grimy brown because we are Indians
woo-woo-woo.
            is your butt wet cold
            mine is

OH MY LOVE

Oh my love oh my love oh my love oh my love oh my love oh my love oh my love oh
my love oh my love oh my love oh my love oh my love oh my love oh my love oh my
love oh my love oh my love oh my love oh my love oh my love oh my love oh my love
oh my love oh my love oh my love oh my love oh my love oh my love oh my love oh
my love oh my love oh my love oh my love oh my love oh my love oh my love oh my
love oh my love oh my love oh my love oh my love oh my love oh my love oh my love
oh my love oh my love oh my love oh my love oh my love oh my love oh my love oh
my love oh my love oh my love oh my love oh my love oh my love oh my love oh my
love oh my love oh my love oh my love oh my love oh my love oh my love oh my love
oh my love oh my love oh my love oh my love oh my love oh my love oh my love oh
my love oh my love oh my love oh my love oh my love oh my love oh my love oh my
love oh my love oh my love oh my love oh my love oh my love oh my love oh my love
oh my love oh my love oh my love oh my love oh my love oh my love oh my love oh
my love oh my love oh my love oh my love oh my love oh my love oh my love oh my
love oh my love oh my love oh my love oh my love oh my love oh my love oh my love
oh my love oh my love oh my love oh my love oh my love oh my love oh my love oh
my love oh my love oh my love oh my love oh my love oh my love oh my love oh my
love oh my love oh my love oh my love oh my love oh my love oh my love oh my love
oh my love oh my love oh my love oh my love oh my love oh my love oh my love oh
my love oh my love oh my love oh my love oh my love oh my love oh my love oh my
love oh my love oh my love oh my love oh my love oh my love oh my love oh my love
oh my love oh my love oh my love oh my love oh my love oh my love oh my love oh
my love oh my love oh my love oh my love oh my love oh my love oh my love oh my
love oh my love oh my love oh my love oh my love oh my love oh my love oh my love
oh my love oh my love oh my love oh my love oh my love oh my love oh my love oh
my love oh my love oh my love oh my love oh my love oh my love oh my love oh my
love oh my love oh my love oh my love oh my love oh my love oh my love oh my love
oh my love oh my love oh my love oh my love oh my love oh my love oh my love oh
my love oh my love oh my love oh my love oh my love oh my love oh my love oh my
love oh my love oh my love oh my love oh my love oh my love oh my love oh my love
oh my love oh my love oh my love oh my love oh my love oh my love oh my love oh
my love oh my love oh my love oh my love oh my love oh my love oh my love oh my
love oh my love oh my love oh my love oh my love oh my love oh my love oh my love
oh my love oh my love oh my love oh my love oh my love oh my love oh my love oh
my love oh my love oh my love oh my love oh my love oh my love oh my love oh my

I AM ON MARS

I am on Mars.
The sun's indifferent.
I am light,
Nominal.
Thin stuff sinuous
On the scabland surface:
I am in Tharsis
Hard by Valles Marineris
Past yardangs of Memnonia
In chaos terrain—
Dark albedos vein your face,
Port-wine disfigured, Eye of Mars,
You saw me from afar,
Lonely, lured me in—
Lot cast, across over
The shrieking silent void I came.
O, to cross the Bridge of Achilles
Past Cape Hera to the Land of Noah—
All under finest fleece,
Shadowless clouds of Olympus Mons.
As billions await transmission
While I, suited, uplink
All I conjure—
The thin stuff of your,
Your summer dress.
It is red, and I,
Golden haired, am in white,
White and gold.

This is an
American Poetry Alliance book.

Look for these other fine APA volumes:

Ram It In
Push Bush

Manly Poetry Just for Men
by Zanzibar "Buck Buck" McFate

**

The Golden Hour
Poems About Death and Other Vital Matters
by Emily Norcross

**

Beastly Bestiary
by A. Tad Strange

Address Correspondence to:
Nadine Sobolevitch, Executive Director
John Sprat, Director of Corporate Giving
Ellen Hastings, Therapist
American Poetry Alliance
MCM, LLC
Box 9881
Chapel Hill, NC 27515-9881

The American Poetry Alliance
Gratefully Acknowledges the Support of Its Benefactors:

Bubang Pusan Group Ltd., Seoul, South Korea
(Maker of Toasters & Other Small Electric Goods),
Mr. and Mrs. Norman D. Bloom of Fountain City, Tennessee,
and al-Yamama Trading Co., Riyadh, Saudi Arabia

Coming Soon:

I BATTLED
A GIANT OTTER
MY GUT BUSTIN', MUTHA LOVIN'
LIFE OF MANLY ADVENTURE

A Tale of
Mad Catastrophe

The Autobiography
of Zanzibar "Buck Buck" McFate

Remember—It's All About Z. Buck!

978-0-595-43911-9
0-595-43911-X

Printed in the United States
81030LV00005B/433-480